ANDERSON WILLIAMS

The Herculaneum papyri

This book was professionally typeset on Reedsy.
Find out more at reedsy.com

Contents

Introduction

The Herculaneum Papyri stand as a unique and invaluable treasure, offering a captivating glimpse into the intellectual and cultural richness of the ancient world. This introduction aims to provide a contextual framework for understanding the significance of these papyri, delving into their discovery, historical background, and the profound impact they have had on classical studies.

Background and Discovery:

The story of the Herculaneum Papyri begins in the mid-18th century when they were unearthed from the ruins of Hercula-neum, a Roman town buried by the eruption of Mount Vesuvius in 79 AD. Unlike the charred scrolls of nearby Pompeii, the Herculaneum scrolls were carbonized due to the intense heat, offering a remarkable level of preservation. This unique set of circumstances has allowed scholars unprecedented access to a wealth of information that might have otherwise been lost to the ages.

Significance of the Herculaneum Papyri:

The significance of the Herculaneum Papyri extends beyond their historical context. These scrolls represent a diverse collection of texts, covering topics ranging from philosophy and poetry to everyday matters. They provide a window into the intellectual pursuits, literary tastes, and social dynamics of the Roman elite in Herculaneum. As a result, the Herculaneum Papyri are not merely artifacts; they are windows into the minds of a bygone era.

Moreover, the Herculaneum Papyri contribute substantially to our understanding of ancient library collections. The Villa of the Papyri, where the scrolls were discovered, is believed to have housed an extensive library, shedding light on the reading habits and intellectual interests of the Roman aristocracy. This discovery challenges preconceived notions about literacy and education in the ancient world.

In the pages that follow, we will embark on a journey to explore the excavation and recovery of these extraordinary artifacts, the challenges faced in deciphering their contents, and the transformative impact they have had on classical scholarship. The Herculaneum Papyri invite us to unravel the mysteries of an ancient library, unlocking a trove of knowledge that continues to captivate scholars and enthusiasts alike.

1

Unearthing the Past

The unfolding of the Herculaneum Papyri saga began in the mid-18th century when the Swiss military engineer Karl Weber, working under the patronage of King Charles III of Spain, initiated the groundbreaking excavations at Herculaneum. Little did Weber and his team anticipate that beneath the layers of volcanic ash lay an ancient library waiting to be rediscovered, a literary time capsule preserved by the catastrophic eruption of Mount Vesuvius in 79 AD.

The meticulous excavation process was not only a testament to the nascent field of archaeology but also a delicate dance with history. As workers carefully unearthed the ruins, they encountered what appeared to be carbonized scrolls. Recognizing the fragility of these artifacts, Weber and his team faced the daunting task of extracting them intact. This process required a delicate balance between precision and patience, as any misstep could lead to irreversible damage to these rare remnants of antiquity.

The recovery of the Herculaneum Papyri presented unique challenges. Unlike traditional paper, the scrolls were made of papyrus, a material susceptible to decay and damage. The carbonization process, a result of the volcanic eruption's intense heat, provided an unexpected layer of protection but also made the scrolls brittle. Early attempts at unfolding the scrolls often resulted in fragments, prompting scholars to explore innovative techniques to reveal the hidden texts without causing irreparable harm.

The Villa of the Papyri:

Central to the discovery of the Herculaneum Papyri is the Villa of the Papyri itself, a luxurious residence that stands as a testament to the grandeur of ancient Roman architecture. Situated on the outskirts of Herculaneum, this opulent villa is believed to have belonged to Lucius Calpurnius Piso Caesoninus, Julius Caesar's father-in-law. Its sprawling layout, adorned with frescoes and mosaics, provides a glimpse into the lifestyle of the Roman elite.

The library, where the majority of the papyri were found, is thought to have been located on the villa's lower level. This space, though partially collapsed, yielded an unparalleled collection of scrolls, hinting at the intellectual pursuits and literary tastes of its inhabitants. The discovery of the Villa of the Papyri challenges conventional notions of Roman literacy, suggesting a sophisticated engagement with written knowledge among the elite, far beyond what was previously imagined.

The excavation and recovery of the Herculaneum Papyri not only revealed a lost library but also opened a doorway to the past, inviting scholars to unravel the secrets preserved in the scrolls. In the subsequent sections, we will delve deeper into the contents of these extraordinary artifacts and the revelations they offer about ancient Roman society and intellectual life

2

The Herculaneum Library

The Herculaneum Library, ensconced within the opulent Villa of the Papyri, emerges as a veritable treasure trove of intellectual wealth, bearing witness to the nuanced literary predilections of the Roman elite during the first century AD. This section invites us to explore the sprawling expanse of this unique collection, unveiling the intricacies of its contents and the profound impact it has had on our understanding of ancient scholarship.

The library's holdings were nothing short of extraordinary. A panoramic view of the scrolls discovered within reveals a rich tapestry of knowledge, where philosophical treatises, poetic compositions, scientific works, and historical narratives intermingled. This diverse array of subjects transcended the boundaries of conventional libraries of the time, attesting to the cultivated tastes and intellectual curiosity of the villa's inhabitants.

Book Types and Subjects:

The Herculaneum Library was a sanctuary of erudition, housing an eclectic mix of literary genres and academic disciplines. Prominently featured were philosophical treatises, notably those of Epicurus, a luminary in Hellenistic philosophy. The inclusion of Epicurean philosophy hinted at a desire for philosophical contemplation, exploring concepts of pleasure, ethics, and the nature of existence. The scrolls, adorned with the thoughts of Epicurus and his followers, offered a window into the philosophical musings that captivated the minds of the Roman aristocracy.

Poetry, too, held a significant place within the library's repertoire. Philodemus, an Epicurean philosopher and poet, contributed to this literary mosaic with verses that traversed themes of love, friendship, and reflections on the natural world. The incorporation of such diverse poetic works suggested a multifaceted appreciation for the arts, underscoring the refined sensibilities of the villa's denizens.

Scientific and technical texts, ranging from medical treatises to mathematical expositions, provided yet another layer of richness to the Herculaneum Library. The scrolls housed within its confines not only reflected the scientific advancements of the time but also hinted at a thirst for knowledge that extended beyond the realms of philosophy and literature. The villa's inhabitants, it seems, were engaged in a holistic pursuit of understanding, embracing disciplines that spanned the breadth of human inquiry.

In essence, the Herculaneum Library transcended its role as a mere repository of texts; it was a testament to the intellectual eclecticism of a society that revered the written word. As we unravel the contents of the Herculaneum Papyri, we embark on a journey through the intellectual landscape of ancient Rome, where the library stands as a beacon illuminating the multifaceted pursuits of knowledge that characterized this remarkable era.

3

Papyrus and Preservation

Material and Production:

At the heart of the Herculaneum Papyri lies the ancient writing material known as papyrus, a botanical wonder that played a pivotal role in the preservation of knowledge. The journey into the intricacies of papyrus begins with the Cyperus papyrus plant, whose fibrous inner layers were meticulously extracted, sliced into thin strips, and meticulously woven into a crisscross pattern. This matrix was then carefully dampened, pressed, and dried, resulting in sheets that could be seamlessly joined to create long, flexible scrolls.

The adoption of papyrus as a writing medium was not merely a matter of convenience; it was a deliberate choice with profound implications for the transmission of classical texts. The lightweight, durable nature of papyrus made it an ideal substrate for writing, facilitating the creation of scrolls that could be easily transported and stored. Its widespread use in the ancient

Mediterranean world marked a significant leap forward in the democratization of knowledge, allowing ideas to traverse geographical and cultural boundaries.

The production of papyrus, therefore, becomes a testament to the ingenuity of ancient civilizations, where the intersection of botanical knowledge and craftsmanship converged to create a material that would shape the course of written communication for centuries.

Challenges in Conservation:

The preservation saga of the Herculaneum Papyri unfolds against the backdrop of both natural disaster and unintended preservation. The eruption of Mount Vesuvius in 79 AD, while causing devastation, inadvertently played a role in carbonizing the scrolls, providing an unusual layer of protection. However, this preservation came with its own set of challenges.

The fragility induced by carbonization meant that the delicate scrolls, when subjected to early attempts at unrolling, often resulted in fragments. The conservationists and scholars faced the delicate task of developing methods that would gently unfurl these scrolls, revealing their contents without causing irreparable damage. It was a meticulous dance between exploration and preservation.

Advanced imaging technologies emerged as indispensable tools in this conservation endeavor. Multispectral imaging and X-ray techniques allowed scholars to peer beneath the layers, deciphering obscured or faded text without physically disrupting the scrolls. The marriage of ancient artifacts with modern technology exemplifies the dynamic synergy between tradition and innovation in the pursuit of unraveling the secrets hidden within these fragile remnants of the past.

Preservation, however, extended beyond the physical artifacts themselves. Initiatives to digitize and catalog the texts not only ensured broader accessibility but also served as a crucial safeguard against potential future deterioration. The evolving landscape of conservation, where traditional techniques harmonize with cutting-edge technologies, underscores the enduring efforts to protect and perpetuate the knowledge encapsulated within the Herculaneum Papyri.

In exploring the materiality of papyrus and the intricacies of its preservation, we embark on a multifaceted journey—a journey that transcends time, weaving together ancient craftsmanship, historical happenstance, and contemporary conservation endeavors. The delicate dance between fragility and resilience, between the tangible and the digital, underscores the profound significance of these artifacts as windows into the intellectual pursuits of a bygone era.

4

Ancient Scrolls Unveiled

The revelation of the Herculaneum Papyri stands as an awe-inspiring intersection of archaeological exploration, technological innovation, and scholarly perseverance. This section invites us to embark on a nuanced exploration of the intricate process involved in unveiling the secrets concealed within these ancient scrolls, traversing the realms of conservation, decipherment, and the profound impact of notable discoveries.

Techniques in Unrolling and Reading:

The fragility of the Herculaneum Papyri, entwined with the consequences of the catastrophic eruption of Mount Vesuvius, necessitated a careful and inventive approach to unraveling the preserved texts. Early attempts at unrolling the scrolls were met with the challenge of brittleness induced by carbonization. To address this, scholars and conservators have historically employed a variety of methods.

The "scroll machine" or "Ercolano machine," a contraption developed in the 18th century, emerged as a groundbreaking tool for controlled and gradual unwinding of the scrolls. This delicate process aimed at minimizing the risk of damage, recognizing the fragile state of these artifacts. In the modern era, imaging technologies, including computed tomography (CT) scanning and synchrotron imaging, have provided non-invasive means to explore the internal structure of the scrolls. These technological advancements have not only facilitated the physical unraveling of the scrolls but have also opened new dimensions for scholarly inquiry.

Moreover, deciphering faded or obscured text became a fascinating challenge in its own right. Multispectral imaging, capable of capturing different wavelengths of light, and other advanced imaging techniques have played a pivotal role in enhancing legibility. These technological strides have not only allowed researchers to virtually unroll and read the texts but have also contributed to a deeper understanding of the language, writing styles, and content embedded in the scrolls.

Notable Discoveries and Texts:

The unveiling of the Herculaneum Papyri has yielded a treasure trove of diverse texts, each contributing to the mosaic of ancient knowledge. Among the notable discoveries is Philodemus's "On Piety," a philosophical treatise that offers insights into ethical considerations within the Epicurean tradition. The presence of this and other Epicurean texts has reshaped our understanding of ancient philosophical discourse, inviting fresh perspectives on ethical and metaphysical inquiries.

The scrolls have also brought to light works attributed to influential figures like Chrysippus, extending the boundaries of classical scholarship. These texts, once buried in the ashes of Vesuvius, have not only contributed to the reconstruction of lost works but have also prompted a reevaluation of historical narratives and philosophical traditions.

The process of unveiling the Herculaneum Papyri represents a collaborative endeavor, with scholars from diverse disciplines working hand in hand. It symbolizes the collective commitment to unlocking the mysteries of the past and reanimating the intellectual legacy of ancient Rome.

In traversing the fascinating journey of ancient scrolls unveiled, we witness not only the meticulous unraveling of texts but also the unfolding of new chapters in our understanding of classical literature, philosophy, and the vibrant intellectual landscape of antiquity. The Herculaneum Papyri, once hidden beneath layers of ash, now stand as eloquent witnesses to the resilience of human curiosity and the enduring quest for knowledge, inviting us to peer through the windows of time into the intellectual pursuits of a bygone era.

5

Insights into Herculaneum Society

The Herculaneum Papyri, woven into the fabric of time, unravel tales of a society that once thrived on the shores of the Bay of Naples. This expansive exploration delves into the scrolls to unearth the layers of ancient Herculaneum society, navigating through the intricate interplay of social dynamics, cultural pursuits, and the minutiae of daily life

Social and Cultural Context:

The diverse range of texts within the Herculaneum Papyri serves as a literary kaleidoscope, offering a nuanced view of the social and cultural milieu of ancient Herculaneum. Positioned as a bustling seaside town, Herculaneum likely teemed with life, commerce, and intellectual exchange. The villa, presumed to be the residence of Lucius Calpurnius Piso Caesoninus, provides a focal point for understanding the opulence and sophistication of the Roman elite who called Herculaneum home.

The breadth of subjects covered in the scrolls—from philosophical treatises to poetic compositions and scientific texts—reflects a society with a rich tapestry of intellectual interests. The presence of Epicurean philosophy in the library speaks to an openness to diverse intellectual currents, suggesting a community that engaged with a broad spectrum of ideas. The cosmopolitan nature of the Roman Empire is echoed in the intellectual eclecticism preserved within the walls of the Villa of the Papyri.

Daily Life Reflected in the Papyri:

Beyond the lofty realms of philosophy and literature, the Herculaneum Papyri cast a revealing light on the daily life of its inhabitants. Interspersed among grand treatises are records of economic transactions, personal letters, and accounts that provide glimpses into the routines and relationships of the society.

Invoices and receipts unearthed from the scrolls document economic transactions, offering insights into trade, commerce, and economic activities. Personal letters, exchanged between family members or friends, provide an intimate look into the familial bonds and personal connections that shaped the social fabric. These artifacts, whether mundane or profound, collectively form a mosaic of daily existence in Herculaneum.

As we traverse the corridors of time through the Herculaneum Papyri, we transcend the conventional understanding of ancient societies. The scrolls elevate the city beyond its architectural remnants, transforming it into a living entity with intellectual vigor, economic vibrancy, and social intricacies. Each text becomes a portal, inviting us to witness not just monumental events but also the pulse of daily life in a city forever etched in history.

The Herculaneum Papyri, as conduits to the past, beckon us to immerse ourselves in the ebb and flow of ancient streets, to overhear conversations, and to witness the interplay of myriad facets of life in a city that met an abrupt yet enduring fate beneath the ashes of Vesuvius.

6

Deciphering the Scripts

The journey into the Herculaneum Papyri extends beyond the realm of preservation and unrolling scrolls; it ventures into the intricate task of deciphering the scripts that lie concealed within the carbonized layers. This section embarks on an extensive exploration of the challenges, methodologies, and scholarly endeavors involved in unraveling the ancient scripts preserved in these extraordinary artifacts.

Writing Systems Used:

The Herculaneum Papyri encompass a variety of writing systems, adding layers of complexity to the decipherment process. The scripts employed in these scrolls are reflective of the linguistic diversity and intellectual influences prevalent in the ancient world.

Epicurean philosophical treatises, for instance, are inscribed in Greek—a language that was a common medium for philosophical discourse in the Hellenistic period. The Greek alphabet, with its nuanced characters and linguistic intricacies, poses both challenges and opportunities for scholars seeking to unlock the philosophical musings embedded in the scrolls.

Moreover, the variety of texts discovered within the Villa of the Papyri includes poetic compositions, scientific works, and other genres, each potentially employing distinct scripts or styles. This rich tapestry of linguistic diversity presents a mosaic that compels scholars to navigate through different linguistic landscapes in their quest to unveil the contents of the scrolls.

Linguistic Challenges and Solutions:

Deciphering the scripts within the Herculaneum Papyri involves grappling with a myriad of linguistic challenges. The carbonization process, while preserving the texts, has also rendered them brittle and prone to damage. This fragility demands a cautious approach to unfolding the scrolls, as any misstep could result in the loss of crucial information.

The faded or obscured nature of the text further complicates the decipherment process. Scholars face the task of reconstructing words and sentences that may have been partially erased or obscured over centuries. This challenge has prompted the integration of advanced imaging technologies, such as multispectral imaging, which can reveal hidden details and enhance legibility without physical manipulation of the fragile scrolls.

Collaborative efforts among linguists, philologists, and historians have played a pivotal role in overcoming these challenges. Comparative analysis with known texts, linguistic expertise, and interdisciplinary collaboration have all contributed to the gradual decipherment of the scripts. The deciphered texts, once elusive behind layers of volcanic residue, now stand as tangible achievements in the ongoing saga of understanding the intellectual wealth contained within the Herculaneum Papyri.

In the grand tapestry of uncovering ancient knowledge, the deciphering of scripts within the Herculaneum Papyri stands as a testament to the tenacity of scholars. It is an intricate dance with linguistic nuances, an artful weaving together of technology and philological expertise, revealing not just the words on ancient parchment but the intellectual legacy of a society preserved for centuries beneath the ashes of Vesuvius.

7

Scholars and Contributions

The decipherment and interpretation of the Herculaneum Papyri have been endeavors undertaken by a dedicated cadre of scholars, whose collective efforts have unveiled the intellectual treasures hidden within these ancient scrolls. This extensive exploration delves into the contributions of scholars, their methodologies, and the transformative impact their work has had on our understanding of classical antiquity.

Pioneering Scholars:

The journey to decipher the Herculaneum Papyri began in the 18th century with scholars who undertook the arduous task of unrolling and preserving the fragile scrolls. Notable among them was Antonio Piaggio, an Italian scholar who developed the "Ercolano machine," a pioneering device designed for the delicate unwinding of the scrolls. His work set the stage for subsequent generations of scholars to build upon his foundations.

In the 20th century, the German philologist and classicist, Wolfgang Schmid, made significant contributions to the study of the Herculaneum Papyri. His expertise in ancient languages and textual criticism laid the groundwork for deciphering and interpreting the contents of the scrolls. Schmid's meticulous work opened avenues for understanding the linguistic intricacies of the texts and paved the way for future scholars to delve deeper into the intellectual legacy of Herculaneum.

Multidisciplinary Collaborations:

The decipherment of the Herculaneum Papyri has been characterized by a multidisciplinary approach, with scholars from diverse fields converging to unlock the mysteries within the scrolls. Linguists, philologists, archaeologists, historians, and conservators have collaborated to bring their unique expertise to the decipherment process.

Advanced imaging technologies have played a crucial role in this collaborative effort. Multispectral imaging, X-ray techniques, and other non-invasive methods have been employed to reveal obscured or faded text, providing scholars with enhanced visibility into the content of the scrolls without causing physical harm.

Contributions to Classical Knowledge:

The contributions of scholars extend beyond the decipherment of individual texts; they have significantly expanded our understanding of classical knowledge. The recovered philosophical treatises, including works by Epicurus and Philodemus, have illuminated the intellectual currents of Herculaneum society. Insights into ancient philosophy, ethics, and metaphysics have been garnered from these recovered texts, challenging and enriching our comprehension of the philosophical landscape of antiquity.

Additionally, the identification of texts attributed to other ancient authors, such as Chrysippus, has broadened the scope of classical scholarship. These rediscovered works contribute not only to the reconstruction of lost texts but also to the reassessment of historical narratives and philosophical traditions.

The work of these scholars has, in essence, transformed the Herculaneum Papyri from enigmatic artifacts into windows offering profound insights into the intellectual pursuits of an ancient society. The ongoing efforts of contemporary scholars ensure that the legacy of Herculaneum continues to be explored, inviting us to appreciate the intricate tapestry of classical knowledge woven into the scrolls hidden for centuries beneath the volcanic remnants of Mount Vesuvius.

8

Digital Approaches to Herculaneum Papyri

In the modern era, digital technologies have become integral tools in the study and preservation of ancient artifacts, including the Herculaneum Papyri. This section delves into the digital approaches employed by scholars, offering a nuanced exploration of how technology has played a transformative role in enhancing accessibility, conservation, and scholarly engagement with these invaluable scrolls.

Digitization for Accessibility:

The digitization of the Herculaneum Papyri has marked a paradigm shift in how these ancient texts are accessed and studied. Digital approaches, such as high-resolution imaging and three-dimensional scanning, have allowed for the creation of virtual replicas that can be explored remotely. This has not only democratized access to the scrolls but has also mitigated the risks associated with physical handling, preserving the fragile artifacts for future generations.

Digital platforms and databases dedicated to the Herculaneum Papyri enable scholars, students, and enthusiasts worldwide to examine the texts, conduct research, and contribute to the collective understanding of these ancient treasures. The democratization of knowledge facilitated by digital accessibility has fostered a global community engaged in the exploration and interpretation of Herculaneum's intellectual legacy.

Advanced Imaging Techniques:

Digital approaches extend beyond traditional imaging methods, incorporating cutting-edge technologies to enhance the legibility of the texts. Multispectral imaging, for instance, captures different wavelengths of light, revealing details and nuances that might escape the human eye. X-ray and tomographic techniques offer non-invasive insights into the internal structure of the scrolls, aiding in the decipherment process.

These advanced imaging technologies not only contribute to the preservation of the Herculaneum Papyri but also unveil hidden layers of information. They play a crucial role in deciphering faded or obscured text, allowing scholars to reconstruct and interpret the content with unprecedented precision. The marriage of digital and archaeological sciences exemplifies the synergy between technology and classical studies.

Computational Analysis and Linguistics:

Digital approaches extend into the realm of computational analysis and linguistics, offering novel methodologies for studying the linguistic features of the Herculaneum Papyri. Computational tools enable scholars to analyze linguistic patterns, syntax, and vocabulary, providing insights into the language used in the scrolls. This interdisciplinary fusion of technology and linguistics contributes to a deeper understanding of the linguistic landscape of ancient Herculaneum.

Moreover, digital platforms facilitate collaborative research, allowing scholars to share datasets, conduct textual analysis, and collectively contribute to decipherment efforts. The dynamic intersection of digital technologies and classical scholarship opens new avenues for exploration, fostering innovation and collaboration in the ongoing study of the Herculaneum Papyri.

In embracing digital approaches, scholars transcend the limitations of physical constraints and embark on a dynamic journey of exploration. The integration of technology not only safeguards the Herculaneum Papyri but also ensures that these ancient texts continue to inspire curiosity and scholarly inquiry in the digital age.

9

Impact on Classical Studies

The discovery, decipherment, and digital exploration of the Herculaneum Papyri have had a profound impact on classical studies, reshaping our understanding of antiquity and enriching the scholarly landscape. This section delves into the far-reaching consequences of the Herculaneum Papyri on classical studies, encompassing diverse facets such as philosophy, literature, linguistics, and our broader comprehension of the ancient world.

Philosophical Resurgence:

The Herculaneum Papyri have sparked a philosophical resurgence, breathing new life into ancient philosophical traditions. The recovered works of Epicurus and Philodemus provide unparalleled insights into Hellenistic philosophy, shedding light on ethical considerations, metaphysical musings, and the philosophical currents that shaped intellectual discourse in the Roman world.

These philosophical texts contribute to ongoing debates within the field of philosophy, prompting scholars to reevaluate the nuances of Epicurean thought and its broader impact on ancient ethical and metaphysical discussions. The Herculaneum Papyri, once lost in the sands of time, have become catalysts for philosophical reexamination and a deeper understanding of the intellectual climate of the ancient Mediterranean.

Literary Rediscovery:

Literary rediscovery is a hallmark of the impact of the Herculaneum Papyri on classical studies. The unearthing of poetic compositions, historical narratives, and scientific treatises within the scrolls has expanded our literary canon from antiquity. Works attributed to Philodemus and others provide glimpses into diverse genres, offering a more comprehensive view of the literary output of ancient Herculaneum.

These literary rediscoveries not only contribute to the reconstruction of lost works but also challenge preconceived notions about the literary landscape of the time. They invite scholars to reassess the literary traditions of ancient Rome, encouraging a nuanced understanding of the interplay between philosophy, poetry, and scientific discourse in the intellectual pursuits of the Roman elite.

Linguistic and Philological Advancements:

Deciphering the scripts within the Herculaneum Papyri has propelled significant advancements in linguistics and philology. The meticulous work of scholars in unraveling the intricacies of Greek writing systems and linguistic features has expanded our understanding of ancient languages. Comparative linguistic analysis, aided by digital tools, has enhanced our grasp of the linguistic nuances embedded in the scrolls.

Moreover, the collaborative efforts of scholars from diverse linguistic backgrounds have fostered a multidisciplinary approach to the study of language in antiquity. The Herculaneum Papyri, as linguistic artifacts, stand as a testament to the rich tapestry of ancient languages and dialects, contributing to broader discussions within the field of linguistics.

Digital Revolution in Classical Scholarship:

The digitization and digital exploration of the Herculaneum Papyri mark a revolutionary chapter in classical scholarship. Digital platforms, virtual replicas, and advanced imaging technologies have democratized access to these ancient texts, transcending geographical boundaries and fostering a global community of scholars and enthusiasts.

The digital revolution has not only increased accessibility but has also facilitated collaborative research. Scholars from diverse disciplines can now engage in real-time discussions, share datasets, and collectively contribute to the decipherment and interpretation of the scrolls. The synergy between classical studies and digital technologies sets a precedent for the dynamic evolution of scholarship in the digital age.

In summary, the impact of the Herculaneum Papyri on classical studies resonates across philosophy, literature, linguistics, and the digital realm. These ancient scrolls, once entombed in volcanic ash, have become catalysts for intellectual revival, prompting scholars to reevaluate, rediscover, and reinterpret the rich intellectual heritage of ancient Herculaneum. As classical studies continue to evolve, the legacy of the Herculaneum Papyri endures as a testament to the enduring fascination and inexhaustible depth of the classical world.

10

Controversies and Debates

The study of the Herculaneum Papyri has not been without its share of controversies and debates, adding layers of complexity to the narrative of their discovery, interpretation, and preservation. This section delves into some of the key controversies and debates that have shaped scholarly discourse surrounding these ancient scrolls.

Ownership and Acquisition:

One enduring controversy revolves around the ownership and acquisition of the Herculaneum Papyri. The initial discovery in the 18th century was part of the excavation of the Villa of the Papyri, owned by the Bourbon monarchy of Naples. However, the circumstances surrounding the acquisition of the scrolls have been subject to historical scrutiny and debate.

Questions regarding the legality of their removal, ownership disputes, and the subsequent dispersion of the scrolls to various institutions have fueled scholarly discussions. The complex history of their acquisition has prompted ethical considerations regarding the responsibilities of custodianship and the rightful ownership of cultural heritage.

Conservation Techniques:

The conservation of the Herculaneum Papyri has been a source of ongoing debate, particularly regarding the techniques employed to preserve and study these delicate artifacts. Early attempts at unrolling the scrolls, sometimes resulting in damage, raised questions about the balance between exploration and preservation.

The introduction of advanced imaging technologies, while revolutionary in enhancing legibility, has also stirred debates. Some scholars argue that digital methods should be employed exclusively to minimize physical manipulation, while others advocate for a holistic approach that combines both traditional conservation methods and cutting-edge technologies.

Authorship Attribution:

The attribution of authorship to specific texts within the Herculaneum Papyri has been a contentious issue. Determining the true authorship of philosophical treatises, poetic compositions, and scientific works is a delicate task, complicated by the fragmentary nature of the scrolls and the challenges of deciphering faded or obscured text.

Scholars have engaged in debates about the authenticity of certain attributions, leading to nuanced discussions about the criteria used for authorship attribution and the reliability of historical sources. The scholarly community continues to grapple with questions surrounding authorship, acknowledging the inherent uncertainties in ascribing texts to specific ancient figures.

Ethical Considerations:

Ethical considerations have emerged as a significant aspect of the controversies surrounding the Herculaneum Papyri. Questions about the responsible custodianship of these cultural artifacts, issues related to repatriation, and concerns about the impact of digital technologies on the preservation of physical manuscripts underscore the ethical dimensions of classical studies.

Debates on whether certain conservation or imaging techniques should be prioritized over others, as well as discussions about open access to digitized versions of the scrolls, reflect broader conversations within the academic and cultural heritage communities about responsible practices in the study and dissemination of ancient artifacts.

In navigating these controversies and debates, scholars strive to strike a delicate balance between preserving the integrity of the Herculaneum Papyri, unraveling their mysteries, and addressing ethical considerations that resonate within the broader field of classical studies and cultural heritage. The ongoing discourse surrounding these ancient scrolls enriches the scholarly dialogue and underscores the multifaceted nature of engaging with the intellectual legacy of the past.

11

Conclusion

In the unfurling tapestry of classical studies, the Herculaneum Papyri stand as enigmatic witnesses to the intellectual vigor and cultural richness of an ancient world forever preserved beneath layers of volcanic ash. From their discovery in the 18th century to the digitized exploration of the 21st, the journey of these fragile scrolls has been one of profound significance, redefining our understanding of antiquity and inspiring ongoing scholarly endeavors.

The Herculaneum Papyri beckon us into a realm where philosophy, literature, and daily life converge in fragments of ancient parchment. Through the delicate dance of decipherment, scholars have breathed life into the philosophical musings of Epicurus, the poetic compositions of Philodemus, and the myriad voices that echo from the ruins of the Villa of the Papyri. These scrolls, once dormant in the shadow of Vesuvius, have become portals inviting us to traverse the avenues of Herculaneum society, to eavesdrop on conversations, and to witness the intellectual pursuits of a bygone era.

Yet, the journey has not been without its controversies, debates, and ethical considerations. From questions of ownership to the ethical use of advanced imaging technologies, the Herculaneum Papyri compel us to grapple with the complexities inherent in the study and custodianship of ancient artifacts. They remind us that the pursuit of knowledge is not devoid of ethical dimensions and that the echoes of the past resonate within contemporary discussions on heritage preservation.

As the scrolls continue to unveil their secrets, the impact on classical studies reverberates across disciplines. They have sparked philosophical resurgences, literary rediscoveries, linguistic advancements, and a digital revolution in scholarship. The Herculaneum Papyri, once relegated to the margins of historical inquiry, now occupy a central stage, contributing to the ongoing narrative of humanity's intellectual evolution.

In conclusion, the Herculaneum Papyri transcend their status as archaeological artifacts; they are windows into the minds of ancient thinkers, into the cultural tapestry of Herculaneum, and into the ongoing dialogue between the past and the present. Their legacy extends beyond the fragility of parchment, reaching into the core of classical studies, where their whispers continue to inspire, challenge, and reshape our understanding of the timeless pursuit of knowledge. The Herculaneum Papyri, in their fragility, resilience, and profound revelations, stand as testament to the enduring quest for intellectual illumination across the ages.